The Little Book
of Curry

THE LITTLE BOOK OF

Curry

ROD GREEN

First published in the United Kingdom in 2001

Text © Rod Green, 2001

First published by Ebury Press
Random House, 20 Vauxhall Bridge Road,
London SW1V 2SA

Random House Australia (Pty) Limited
20 Alfred Street, Milsons Point, Sydney,
New South Wales 2061, Australia

Random House New Zealand Limited
18 Poland Road, Glenfield, Auckland 10, New Zealand

Random House South Africa (Pty) Limited
Endulini, 5a Jubilee Road, Parktown 2193, South Africa

Random House Group Limited Reg. No. 954009

www.randomhouse.co.uk

A CIP catalogue record for this book is available from the British Library.

24681097531

ISBN 0 09 187956 6

Printed and bound in Denmark by Nørhaven A/S

Thanks to The Bombay Restaurant in Ewell, Surrey, whose delivery people always tap gently on the window instead of ringing the doorbell so as not to wake the baby

INTRODUCTION

When Shah Jehan's wife, Mumtaz-i-Mahal, died, he decided to build a magnificent mausoleum at Agra in India in her memory. It was named the Taj Mahal. Little did Shah Jehan know that more than 350 years later there would be a Taj Mahal in the High Street of almost every major town in Britain. The British versions may fall some way short of the magnificence of the original, but the proliferation of Indian restaurants is proof positive of the great and enduring passion the British have for curry.

A passion for curry? Passion? Does curry really merit the sort of language usually reserved for affairs of the heart? It does according to Professor Stephen Gray of Nottingham Trent University. Professor Gray's research indicates that the taste of curry sends blood pressure and heart rates rocketing and that even the thought of a favourite Indian dish is enough to stimulate the sort of biological responses more likely to be experienced *en route* to a hot date than a hot meal. 'We see an increase in blood pressure and heart rate that is similar to sexual arousal,' the Professor maintains.

The British love affair with Indian food is not, however, a new phenomenon. As one might expect, the romance began when India lay at the heart of the British

Empire rather then somewhere in the digestive tract. As long ago as 1845, Eliza Acton's cookery book *Modern Cookery For Private Families* included a recipe for 'A Common Indian Currie', although it wasn't until 1911 that the Salut-e-Hind, Britain's first Indian restaurant, opened in Holborn in London.

Nowadays, curries come in every conceivable form, from expensive, award-winning dishes served in the choicest of restaurants, to pre-packed, frozen TV dinners which can be whacked into the microwave and wolfed down by the time the teams trot out for the second half.

Curries and 'Indian' restaurants have become the butt of countless jokes, and this book will do nothing to change that.

If we Brits didn't adore what we call 'a curry', then we wouldn't spend so much time in curry houses and we wouldn't have much to say about curry at all. But we do adore it. It is a passion.

The Little Book of Curry is, like a good curry, here to be enjoyed, intended to be savoured by the gourmet as much as it is for those who believe that the correct wine to drink with a curry is a lager tops. Just don't drop it on your trousers.

WHY NOT START WITH PAPPADAMS? DOESN'T EVERYONE?

Pappadams are mass produced in this country, quick-dried and factory packed. The choicest pappadams, though, are sun dried in India. They can be made from chickpeas, rice flour, tapioca, potato flour or lentil flour and are scattered on huge outdoor drying floors to dry naturally in the sunshine. They have been made that way for more than a thousand years.

Next time you're slopping mango chutney all over your pappadam, pause to reflect on the fact that you are about to savour a wafer-thin slice of history.

So what is a curry? The curry bush grows all over India and flowers in the spring with huge steaming plates of chicken dhansak hanging from its branches. Sadly, that's not true; it actually looks a bit like a bay tree and its leaves have been used for centuries in dishes from southern India. That's not where the term 'curry' comes from, though. The word probably originates from kaari, which in some areas means a spicy vegetable dish and elsewhere can be a meat dish, both likely to be served with rice.

Karhi, on the other hand, is a thick, creamy spicy vegetarian dish in the Punjab. It is sometimes also taken simply to mean 'sause'.

What we commonly refer to as 'a curry'

is a generic term adopted by the British to cover almost any spicy Indian food cooked in a sauce. Whatever the origins of the word, Indians certainly never used it as a 'catch-all' to categorise their food the way the British have done.

Needless to say, you can't grow a beautiful curry shrub by planting a king prawn madras in your window box.

A FEW THINGS THAT MIGHT TURN UP ON A CURRY HOUSE MENU

A is for . . .

Aloo	potato
Achar	pickle
Adrak	ginger

Those of you who have been paying attention will have noticed that aloo means potato. You're probably now thinking, 'Aha! That means vindaloo must have lots of potato in it!' Good guess, but not quite right. Vindaloo comprises of the word for vinegar (vin) and the aloo bit is from the Portuguese word for garlic.

Curry Is Good For You!

Who on earth in history first thought,
'I know . . . these chilli things burn my
mouth so much they loosen my teeth,
the hotter ones just about blow my
head off, and the next day I wouldn't
wish my arsehole on my worst
enemy . . . let's find lots of ways to
cook with them.'

He must have been daft as a duck.
Madder than a Maharajah's mallard.
Or was he?

Heavily spiced food helped to make some pretty unpalatable things ultimately edible, but the purgative effects of strong spices and chillies clearing out the system were also thought to be a good thing, especially in a land like India where a good clear-out might rid you of the sort of stomach bugs and parasites that could cause you severe health problems in the long term.

Different spices are believed to have different beneficial properties, as you will see when you read further.

Fish and chips has always been thought of as traditional British fare but Indian restaurants now cook twice as much food as fish and chip shops. There are almost 10,000 Indian restaurants in the UK, making it the Brits' favourite food fad by far.

London is estimated to have around 3,500 Indian restaurants.

Worcestershire Sauce . . . English?
No, Indian. Lord Sandys had been
Governor of Bengal before he returned
home to Worcester in 1835 with a taste
for curry and a recipe for a spicy
condiment. He gave his recipe to two
chemists, Mr Lea and Mr Perrins, and
they produced a quantity of the sauce
which everyone agreed was . . .
truly disgusting. The unsuccessful
brew was left languishing in a cellar for
a year before someone was brave
enough to try it again. Surprise,
surprise, having been 'laid down' for a
year, it turned out to be quite palatable.
The sauce was unleashed on the
general public in 1837.

The honour of being Britain's longest-serving curry house goes to Veeraswamy in Regent Street in London.
It first began spicing up the lives of its clientele in 1926.

Chillies are first known to have been
cultivated in South America more than
9,000 years ago. Had they been
named by the first person to taste one,
they would probably have been called
'lagerquicks'.

Although they are generally referred to as 'Indian' restaurants, over 80% of curry houses in the UK are actually run by Bangladeshis.

'Fancy a Ruby on the way home?'
Curry is now such an integral part of
the British lifestyle that it even has its
own rhyming slang term. The late
Ruby Murray was the singer whose
name came top of the bill. It obviously
rhymes with curry but also has the
'ruby' element and the jewel's close
association with India.

Gladys Murray, Stella Murray or any
other such name just wouldn't have
worked as well, would it?

A FEW THINGS THAT MIGHT TURN UP ON A CURRY HOUSE MENU

B is for . . .

Bhaji	fried
Bhindi	okra or ladies' fingers
Batak	duck

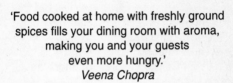

'Food cooked at home with freshly ground
spices fills your dining room with aroma,
making you and your guests
even more hungry.'
Veena Chopra

The Curry House Top Twenty Hit Singles

1. Pappadam Preach — **Madonna**
2. Gimme Gimme Gimme A Naan After Midnight — **Abba**
3. Leader Of The Pakura — **Shangri-las**
4. Bhaji Trousers — **Madness**
5. Tears On My Pilau — **Johnny Nash**
6. Paperback Raita — **The Beatles**
7. What's Become Of The Bloke That Farted? — **Colin Blunstone**
8. Korma Chameleon — **Kulcha Club**
9. Stand By Your Naan — **Tammy Wynette**
10. It's My Chapati And I'll Karai If I Want To — **Dave Stewart & Barbara Gaskin**

11. Girlfriend In A Korma — **The Smiths**
12. Sag Aloo Wave Gobi — **Soft Cell**
13. Steam From Mulligatawny — **Diana Ross**
14. Chana Girl — **David Bowie**
15. Dhansak Queen — **Abba**
16. Vindaloo Sunset — **The Kinks**
17. Tikka To Ride — **The Beatles**
18. Dhansak In The Dark — **Bruce Springsteen**
19. No Bhuna No Karai — **Bob Marley**
20. Jalfrezi For You — **Madonna**

Many towns stake a claim to being Britain's 'Curry Capital' outside London including Manchester, Birmingham, Leicester and Bradford. Bradford certainly boasts a wide range of high-quality eateries with over 250 curry houses. Only three of these are Indian restaurants. The rest are owned and managed by Pakistanis, serving dishes which are subtly different from Indian cooking, enjoying added influences from Pakistan's neighbours in the Middle East.

'Of all the beans, the mung bean is the
one that causes the least flatulence.'
Madhur Jaffrey

HOT AND HORNY!
Sex And The Curry

It's a well-known fact that eating a
curry makes you incredibly randy –
or is that just me? In any case,
many common curry ingredients have
long been regarded as aphrodisiacs.

Ginger is believed to stimulate your
hormones and has, historically, been
held as a potent aphrodisiac
throughout India.

Two Indian restaurants in London, The Tamarind in Mayfair and Zaika in Fulham Road were recently awarded their first and much coveted Michelin stars. The Tamarind includes such exotic delicacies as tandoori quail kebabs on its menu, although chef Vineet Bhatia of the Zaika admitted that he had 'never cooked a curry in his life'.

You might think that Vindaloo is about as Indian as curries come but you'd be wrong. With the Indians' talent for adapting recipes and their inevitable innovative flair, they were almost bound to pull the naan over your eyes.

So where does Vindaloo come from? Want to phone a friend? If you had said Portugal, you'd have been right. Vindaloo was adopted by the Goans via their trading links with the Portuguese, adapted to accommodate local ingredients and added to all of the best curry house menus.

CURRY IS GOOD FOR YOU!

Spices that are positively healthy

Turmeric – related to ginger and looking fairly similar as far as the root part is concerned, turmeric is dried and crushed into a powder which gives a dish a substantial yellow colour. It can also be used to produce a yellow dye.

Turmeric is regarded in India as a kind of digestive to help a large meal pass through peacefully.

Food cooked and eaten in India is
vastly different from the sort of dishes
we associate with India and, broadly
speaking, the major differences in
Indian cuisine are regional. Chillies are
more widely used in the south, nuts
and yoghurt feature more prominently
in the north, fish and spices are typical
in the east and foreign influences
(as with the aforementioned vindaloo)
are more common in the west.

'Cooking without spices is like painting
without colour.'
Sybil Kapoor

Beef, lamb and seafood are always popular options on curry house menus but chicken is generally dominant. This reflects the fact that, in many parts of India, chicken is regarded as the premier meat, served on special occasions or when guests are being entertained.

HOT AND HORNY!
Sex And The Curry

Nutmeg, if taken in sufficient
quantities, is thought to have a
hallucinogenic effect. While that might
leave you all limp and lifeless, it is also
believed to help gentlemen remain
firmly upright.

The Indian influence on the UK food industry is now huge with over 60,000 people employed in producing Indian meals either in restaurants or in factories, creating an estimated turnover of around £1.8 billion.

That's a lot of biryanis.

A FEW THINGS THAT MIGHT TURN UP ON A CURRY HOUSE MENU

C is for . . .

Chana	chickpeas
Chapli	a kind of pot or frying pan
Chingri	prawn

There are over 36,000 curry-related
websites in the UK and Ireland alone.
You can order food to be delivered, order
ingredients to cook Indian meals yourself,
find recipes for your favourite food,
check out restaurants in a particular
area or even contribute your own
restaurant reviews.

While you spend the evening doing all
that, though, your usual table at the local
balti house will be pining
for you . . .

The Curry Monster website includes a recipe for their Chicken Ringstinger. As you might imagine, this is not a dish for the fainthearted or for anyone who might spend any part of the next day less than five panicked paces from the nearest loo.

Although curry powder is often regarded as something of a convenience 'cheat' in Indian cooking as it is a blend of spices (including curry leaves) which might normally be added individually to the dish as part of the recipe, many Indian women do pre-prepare and store their own spice mixtures.

Beware if you aren't up to handling a curry of vindaloo strength and spot the gentler-sounding Bindaloo or Tindaloo on a menu. They're the same thing.

HOT AND HORNY!
Sex And The Curry

Onions might not at first seem to be a
particularly sexy food. After all, who
wants to snog an onion-breath?
They are, however, recommended for
their aphrodisiac qualities in
ancient Hindu texts.

If onions really are the food of lurrrrrrrrrrve, then the curry that will really get you in the mood is a dopiaza. Do means 'two' and piaza is 'onions', meaning that you get twice the amount of the lurrrrrrrrrrve globes in a dopiaza.

Dopiaza – the lurrrrrrrrrrve curry.

The Agra chain of restaurants in the York area liven up their diners' evening out from time to time by providing a spot of entertainment in the shape of Basil Fawlty and Manuel lookalikes.

This certainly makes dining out a truly multicultural experience with an English hotelier beating up a Spanish waiter in an Indian restaurant.

A FEW THINGS THAT MIGHT TURN UP ON A CURRY HOUSE MENU

D is for . . .

Dhal	lentils
Dahi	yoghurt
Dhania	coriander

Curry Is Good For You!

Spices that are positively healthy

Saffron – the plant is a kind of crocus and, although used in biryanis and kormas, it's actually quite expensive, costing around £100 per ounce. Don't think you can just heave a few crocuses out of that roundabout on the ring road to flog to your local curry house.
You need over 70,000 plants to make just a pound of saffron.

A sort of 'saffron tea' is said to be a good cure for headaches and hangovers (good for a bloke after a boozy night out) and to help bring on menstruation (not so good for a bloke after a boozy night out).

The National Curry Chef of the Year is an award sponsored by food manufacturer Patak's and started out as a way of improving co-operation between Bradford's environmental health department and Asian restaurant owners. Since 1995 the competition has been nationwide and the current title holder is Ranjeet Singh of the Passage To India restaurant in Middlesex. Previous winners have been Manzoor Ahmed of the Tabaq, London (who came top in 1999 and 1998), Simon Morris of Grafton Manor in Worcester (1997), Abdhul Moner of Mem Saheb on Thames, London (1996) and Rois Ali of the Rupali Restaurant in Coventry (1995).

Garam masala is the main spice
mixture used in Indian cooking.
In rough translation it means
'hot mixture'. Every Indian cook will
have his or her own slightly different
recipe for garam masala but the basic
ingredients vary very little.

Curry fanatics in the UK need not only cook curry, talk about curry, visit curry websites, eat and breathe curry, they can also go and live there. The village of Curry Rivel in Somerset is but a stone's throw from its neighbour North Curry. North Curry consists of just one main street with a central square known as The Pepper Pot.

TOP TWENTY INGREDIENTS IN INDIAN COOKING

(Alphabetical order)

Bay leaves	Garlic
Cardamom	Ginger
Chillies	Mustard seeds
Cinnamon	Nigella seeds
Cloves	Onion seeds
Coriander	Peppercorns
Cumin	Saffron
Curry (powder & leaves)	Sesame seeds
Fennel	Tamarind
Fenugreek seeds	Turmeric

A FEW THINGS THAT MIGHT TURN UP ON A CURRY HOUSE MENU

E is for . . .

Egg   well of
                       course it is

Elaichee   cardamom

Hot And Horny!
Sex And The Curry

Rosemary has a delightfully fresh scent but it is also thought to have an effect on the nervous system and increase the blood circulation resulting in outrageous randiness.

'Spam curry is really nice
with pitta bread.'
Manju Mahli

Tandoori dishes are so called because they are baked in a tandoor, which is traditionally a charcoal-fired, clay-lined oven that cooks at incredibly high temperatures. The red colour comes from the spices used but is also commonly enhanced by flavourless food colouring.

Running through the list of dishes on the menus in different curry houses you will see an enormous variation in the spelling of certain things. Is it korma, qorma, kurma or khorma? None of them is right. And none of them is wrong. There is simply no straightforward way to translate into English and the Roman alphabet from the languages and dialects of the Indian subcontinent.

So don't slag off the waiter unless you want a dooppee atsa in your lap.

CURRY IS GOOD FOR YOU!

Spices that are positively healthy

Pepper – peppercorns grow as little berries in tropical forests in India. The different colours of peppercorns depend on when the berries were harvested. They start off green, then turn orange and red. Black peppers are berries that have been left to ripen and dry. White peppers are ripened berries peeled and then dried.

Pepper makes you sneeze, so it has been used to clear the nasal passages, but it also helps us to digest rich food and avoid constipation, thus clearing various other passages. It is also said to help improve the memory but I can't remember who said it. Pass the pepper.

Food manufacturer Patak's has become one of the great success stories of the British food industry. Based in Lancashire, they not only supply a vast range of ingredients for the home market, but for the last 25 years they have been exporting worldwide and now reach over 40 countries.

A FEW THINGS THAT MIGHT TURN UP ON A CURRY HOUSE MENU

F is for . . .

Firni   rice-based dessert

More   I wanted to put more in here but there is no f in more*

*sounds really funny if you say it aloud, honest.

Strangest-sounding curry dish ever?
What about Chicken Lollipop Masala,
produced by Ranjeet Singh
in his successful bid for the
National Curry Chef of the Year (2000) title.

Recent figures estimated that at least
2.5 million people eat at a curry house
each week. Must be a bugger to
get served there.

HOT AND HORNY!
Sex And The Curry

Mustard has a reputation for stimulating the sex glands and at one time hardy gents with too much time on their hands used to rub it all over their bodies to try to make themselves irresistible to the opposite sex.

Surely a box of milk tray and a bottle of plonk would have worked a bit better?

At one time The Red Fort in London's Soho laid claim to being the only restaurant in the country cooking authentic Indian food. Now it has the distinction of supplying the Prime Minister Tony Blair with his takeaways.

A FEW THINGS THAT MIGHT TURN UP ON A CURRY HOUSE MENU

G is for . . .

Gosht	meat
Gobi	cauliflower
Ghee	clarified butter

The range and quality of curries and 'Indian' food available in the UK is constantly expanding along with the proportion of our population with Indian, Pakistani and Bangladeshi roots, now estimated at around 5% of the total population.

Rubbing with vinegar can remove
curry stains from your carpet.

THE HOT TOP TWENTY

The following dishes have been placed
in order of ferocity from the Phal,
which some restaurants won't even
serve in case some poor sod is
persuaded to order it without knowing
what he's about to do to himself, to the
pleasant and harmless Muglai.
Different restaurants and different
chefs will, of course, prepare food
differently, so the order could change
according to where you eat.

1. Phal
2. Vindaloo
3. Ceylon
4. Jalfrezi
5. Madras
6. Balti
7. Pathia
8. Korai
9. Dansak
10. Rogan Josh
11. Methi
12. Dopiaza
13. Bhuna
14. Korma
15. Palok
16. Jeera
17. Makon
18. Kashmiri
19. Malayan
20. Muglai

CURRY IS GOOD FOR YOU!

Spices that are positively healthy

Onions – more of a vegetable than a spice perhaps, but widely used in Indian cooking either as a grown up onion or as onion seeds.

Medicinal properties? Well, onions boiled to a pulp can be made into a poultice for treating boils and chilblains. Chopping an onion makes you cry, of course, so it's good if you've got something in your eye that you want to wash out. No, don't go rubbing raw onion on your eyeball! Just peel or slice an onion, and let the vapours it gives off do their job naturally.

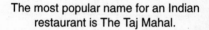

The most popular name for an Indian
restaurant is The Taj Mahal.

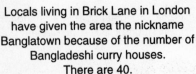

Locals living in Brick Lane in London have given the area the nickname Banglatown because of the number of Bangladeshi curry houses.
There are 40.

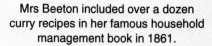

Mrs Beeton included over a dozen curry recipes in her famous household management book in 1861.

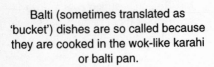

Balti (sometimes translated as 'bucket') dishes are so called because they are cooked in the wok-like karahi or balti pan.

Eating curry can help you lose weight.
Well, not if you stuff yourself with too
much of it, but chillies are known to
stimulate your metabolism and as such
they can be seen as a slimming aid.

Chillies are also thought to be good for asthma, arthritis, blood clots and shingles – remember that next time you chomp on a habanero and your ears drop off.

A FEW THINGS THAT MIGHT TURN UP ON A CURRY HOUSE MENU

H is for . . .

Haldi	turmeric
Halwa	sweet dish, although not always a dessert
Hari	green

Curry lovers often refer to themselves
as curry addicts or curryholics, but can
they really be addicted? Perhaps.
The hot peppers used in some curries
contain capsaicin, a chemical that
stimulates the brain to produce
endorphins. This can create a kind of
'curry high' and induce a feeling of
well-being that might
certainly become addictive.

HOT AND HORNY!
Sex And The Curry

Chillies, it would appear, are good for just about everything. They contain Vitamins A, E and C as well as potassium and folic acid. The capsaicin they release into your body is also believed to act as a stimulant and aphrodisiac.

Ladies, if you are pregnant and suffering from morning sickness, a curry is probably the last thing you want, especially if a night out and a curry is what got you in that state in the first place. In fact, since your baby feeds entirely from you, hot, spicy food isn't really a good idea. By the time you're ready to give birth, though, and the little blighter doesn't want to come out, a good curry can persuade him otherwise. Curries are known to help induce childbirth.

A FEW THINGS THAT MIGHT TURN UP ON A CURRY HOUSE MENU

I is for . . .

| Imli | tamarind |
| Ick | get the waiter to wipe it off |

You might think that your tolerance of fiery hot spices is second to none and that you can wolf down the hottest of curries regardless of any cunningly disguised chillies or peppers that are lurking in the sauce somewhere, but you would be hard pressed to match the achievements of the world champion chilli muncher. At a chilli eating contest held in the Philippines in 1999 Eriberto N Gonzales Jr munched his way through 350 chillies in just 3 minutes. He then went straight to the loo, there was a blast like a sonic boom and Eriberto was discovered wandering dazed on the M1 just outside Northampton.

How come some people seem to be able to eat the hottest dish on the menu, munch their way through every chilli on the plate and wash it all down with a pint of Tabasco and a Worcester sauce chaser, while the mere thought of a madras sends others screaming towards the lavs? Some of us have a higher concentration of taste buds in our mouths than others, making us more sensitive.

You can condition yourself by starting off with a mild curry and building up over a period of time to the real scorchers but that takes courage, dedication and a cast iron arse.

An Oxford-based company has applied
for a patent for a new drug using curry
ingredients, which, they believe,
can be used in food to help prevent
bowel cancer.

A FEW THINGS THAT MIGHT TURN UP ON A CURRY HOUSE MENU

J is for . . .

Jingha	prawn
Jaiphul	nutmeg
Jaivitri	mace

You can rate the fiery effects of curry in any number of ways, from innocent to incendiary, from tasty to terrifying or from sublime to 'I'll buy that half of lager off you for a tenner!!'

A German scientist, however, has come up with a more precise measurement – for chillies at least. Herman Scoville's modestly named Scoville Scale is based on the capsaicin content of peppers and works out roughly as follows.

Bell pepper	0 Scovs
Cascabell	1,500 – 2,500 Scovs
Jalapeno	2,500 – 5,000 Scovs
Cayenne	30,000 – 50,000 Scovs
Habanero	100,000 – 500,000 Scovs

Although traditionally thought to be the most devastatingly fiery of all peppers, the habanero has been overtaken by a new variety from growers in northern India. The tezpur is said to be rated at 850,000 Scovs.

CURRY IS GOOD FOR YOU!

Spices that are positively healthy

Ginger – indispensable in Indian cooking, ginger is used in just about everything.

Feeling a bit Moby Dick? Ginger gets your juices going and helps to settle your stomach.

Feeling a bit bunged up? Ginger helps to soothe coughs and colds and clears your head.

Feeling a bit bubonic? Ginger has antiseptic properties that have been used to treat all sorts of ailments, including the plague!

A FEW THINGS THAT MIGHT TURN UP ON A CURRY HOUSE MENU

K is for . . .

Karahi pan	wok-like pan
Karhai	stir-fried
Khari	sauce

The world record for curry
consumption goes to an unexploded
Uxbridge man who, up to June of
2000, had eaten 2.5 tonnes
of the stuff.

In 1998 the Ray restaurant in Maldon, Essex produced a curry weighing in at almost 6,000lbs or over 13,000 portions – enough to serve as a starter for our friend from Uxbridge.

Hot And Horny!
Sex And The Curry

Roses are the most romantic flower of
all and they have been used in love
potions ever since the girl first said,
'A rose? But won't I cut myself on the
thorns?' and the boy said,
'Well, you might feel a little prick . . .'

So what do they have to do with curry?
Rose petals are widely used in Indian
cooking. Rosewater is a key ingredient
of kheer, a speciality rice dish served
as a dessert on very special
occasions.

A FEW THINGS THAT MIGHT TURN UP ON A CURRY HOUSE MENU

L is for . . .

Lehsun	garlic
Lal mirch	red chillies
Loki	marrow

Until the rules on where a marriage
ceremony could take place were
relaxed (especially in Scotland)
The Brilliant restaurant in Southall was
the only curry house in the country
where you could actually get married.

'Do you, Shirley, take this naan . . .'

CURRY IS GOOD FOR YOU!

Spices that are positively healthy

Nigella seeds – used in a range of vegetable and fish recipes but also found in some chicken and meat dishes. They are also a common ingredient in pickles.

Ladies, do you yearn for a fuller figure? Do you long to see a man sneak a peek down the front of your dress and see more than just your shoes? Forget expensive breast implants. Eating nigella seeds improves the shape and increases the size of women's breasts. It comes as no surprise, therefore, that it is also said to stimulate the production of breast milk.
No guarantees, no refunds.

In Manchester, curry enthusiasts flock to what they call the 'Curry Mile'. There are more than 60 eateries in the neighbourhood.

In a balti restaurant the food can be
cooked to your own specifications,
customised and personalised just for you.
You can ask for your meal to be as hot and
spicy as you like and even specify your
own combinations of meat and vegetables.
Don't take that as a licence to order the
first thing that comes into your head.
There's always some clever dick who'll ask
for elephant's trunk, or tiger's tail,
or bison testicles, or . . .

A FEW THINGS THAT MIGHT TURN UP ON A CURRY HOUSE MENU

M is for . . .

Mirch	chillies
Murgh	chicken
Mutar	peas

If you decide to cook your own curry,
be careful when handling chillies.
Rather than using your bare hands,
wear rubber gloves, and don't let
chillies anywhere near any
cuts or grazes – it will sting like you've
been thrashed naked with the stingiest
nettles in stingydom. For similar
reasons, always wash your hands
afterwards, avoid scratching that itch in
your eye or picking your nose and
gents, make sure you've scrubbed
your hands at least twice before you
whip the old man out for a pee.

Nothing beats sitting down to eat in a proper Indian nosherie, but 'Free delivery within a ten mile radius' comes close. Some people can take the delivery service a bit too far, though. Rachel Kerr, from Newcastle, just couldn't live without a takeaway from her favourite Indian restaurant, the Rupali. She ordered her naan bread, vegetable biryani, rice, pappadams and pickles via the internet and took delivery four days later on Sydney Harbour Bridge in Australia where she was travelling at the time. The order was seen as an irresistible challenge by the Newcastle-based website which organised the internet ordering service. There's no truth in the rumour that they had to go back because they forgot the naan.

CURRY IS GOOD FOR YOU!

Spices that are positively healthy

Mustard seeds – black and red mustard seeds are commonly used in Indian cookery in fish and vegetable recipes as well as in pickles.

Mustard seeds contain, among other things, sulphur and will make you puke your guts up. The polite term for this is an 'emetic'.

Mustard mixed with hot water and applied as a poultice draws blood to the surface of the skin, which can have a soothing effect.
It has also been used as a poultice on the chests of those with bronchitis.

For those who suffer with their feet, mustard in hot water makes an excellent foot bath.

A FEW THINGS THAT MIGHT TURN UP ON A CURRY HOUSE MENU

N is for . . .

Nargis	boiled egg
Namak	salt
Nargal	coconut milk

TOP TEN TERMS FOR POST CURRY SHITS DISORDER

1. Delhi Belly
2. Bombay Bum
3. Burning Ring of Fire
4. Ruby's Revenge
(Ruby Murray = Curry)
5. Tandoori Trots
6. Bangalore Buttocks
7. Custer's Last Stand (the Indians got him in the end)
8. Bengali Bottom Trumpet
9. Karachi Crack
10. Mysore Arse

The dish most regularly ordered in Britain's curry houses is Chicken Tikka Masala. Ironically, this is not an exotic recipe created for the tables of Maharajas or red-faced colonial colonels. It was devised in this country by Bangladeshi cooks purely to cater for the British tastebuds.

Double irony – Chicken Tikka Masala has now been exported and can be found on restaurant menus in India.

A case of coals to Newcastle – or parathas to the Punjab if you prefer.

CURRY IS GOOD FOR YOU!

Spices that are positively healthy

Garlic – widely used in any number of curry dishes, garlic is hugely beneficial to your health.Eating garlic is thought to help prevent colds and stomach bugs as it has an antiseptic effect. It's also believed to help ease flatulence, although given the smell that garlic can leave on your breath you have to wonder which end is worse. Tough choice. Garlic is also a good natural insecticide for the garden. It reduces the insect population as male insects are greatly attracted to it but when they come to mate you can hear hundreds of squeaky little female midge voices all over the garden screaming, 'Not bloody likely, dog-breath!' Maybe not, but it is a natural insecticide. No need to mention vampires, I suppose.

A Wolverhampton restaurant boasts one of the most unusual curry dishes ever – kangaroo balti. Naz Islam, who runs the restaurant, took a trip to Australia, spotted kangaroo on a couple of menus and decided to offer it as a treat for homesick Ozzies.

A FEW THINGS THAT MIGHT TURN UP ON A CURRY HOUSE MENU

O is for . . .

Okra   vegetable
                    (also bhindi and
                    ladies' fingers)

If you eat a hot chilli by accident, as an experiment, for a dare or because you're just stupid, you may think that you've got away with it for a couple of seconds, then reality kicks in with a vengeance. Vesuvius erupts somewhere in the back of your mouth, your tonsils are toasting like you've just swallowed a three-bar electric fire and your eyeballs are suffering a meltdown that makes Chernobyl seem about as hot as an ice cube in a snowman's Y-fronts.

Lager will not help. Neither will water, wine or lemonade.

The only things which will help to ease the burning sensation are dairy products such as yoghurt, milk or ice cream.
That's why those clever Indians have dishes like raita.

Unlike the burning that curries can cause in the mouth, there's no real anti-dote for Karachi Crack. Yoghurt might work in the mouth but there's no use in ramming it up your Khyber, although some of you might enjoy trying it . . .

Many Indian dishes include things that aren't really meant to be eaten – especially chillies. Cinnamon sticks, bay leaves and other sundry items can turn up on your plate and that's where they're meant to stay. In India, people recognise those things that are there for flavouring only and it is perfectly acceptable to move them to the side of the plate while you finish the rest of your meal.

CURRY IS GOOD FOR YOU!

Spices that are positively healthy

Fenugreek seeds – a commonly used ingredient in curry powders but the leaves can also be used in salads and have plenty of Vitamin A and C as well as calcium and iron.

A poultice can be made from the seeds to treat inflamed skin while a kind of tea made from the leaves is good for colds and as a general pick-me-up. This can also help encourage lactation in mothers with new-born babies.

A FEW THINGS THAT MIGHT TURN UP ON A CURRY HOUSE MENU

P is for . . .

Paneer	cheese
Palok	spinach
Poori	a type of bread

On any evening out with friends, you'll always come across one vindaloony (invariably a bloke) who boasts he can eat the strongest curry they can serve up on a plate without dissolving the china.

Try him on a phal. A phal will sort him out. If it doesn't leave him in tears with a face like the backside of a barbary ape, then he hasn't got any feeling in his mouth anyway.

Recipe books and cookery programmes on the telly are all very well, but, unless you are Indian, Pakistani or Bangladeshi and learn the art of traditional cooking as it is passed down from one generation to the next (and then learn how to cook all the stuff us Brits *think* is real Indian food), you've no chance to learn about the finer points of curry cooking – or do you? Thames Valley University now boasts a very successful Academy of Asian Culinary Arts. At last there's a Uni course you can get your teeth into!

The largest naan you are likely to
come across is a table naan,
which looks like an elephant sat on it
and is served in some balti restaurants
where, of course, you should eat by
scooping up your food with the naan
rather than using knives and forks.

A FEW THINGS THAT MIGHT TURN UP ON A CURRY HOUSE MENU

Q is for . . .

Qeema	minced meat
	(also keema)
Qorma	mild, creamy sauce
	(also Korma)
Qulfi	ice cream
	(also kulfi)

Curry Is Good For You!

Spices that are positively healthy

Fennel – the seeds are used in a variety of dishes but also roasted to be eaten at the end of a meal to cleanse the palate.

Another ingredient with a whole host of medicinal uses, fennel can be used as a skin cleanser or in face packs but has also been held by various cultures to be an antidote for snake venom, to aid digestion, to work as a painkiller, to improve the eyesight and to give you courage.

Like garlic, it was also believed to ward off evil spirits, especially witches.

UK curryholics spend an estimated £5.5 million per day on their favourite nosh – that's £5.5 million between us, not each.

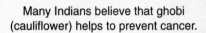

Many Indians believe that ghobi
(cauliflower) helps to prevent cancer.

Curryholics sit down to tuck in to yet another fiery feast on such a regular basis now that even the Tourist Board agrees they are boosting the humble curry to the status of National Dish – except in Hull. In Hull there are three times as many Chinese takeaways as there are Indian nosheries.

CURRY IS GOOD FOR YOU!

Spices that are positively healthy

Cumin – cumin seeds both white and black are used both whole and ground in a number of curry dishes as well as in pilau rice.

Cumin is another of the spices which helps to relieve flatulence and can also be used to concoct a tonic for chest colds and as a poultice treatment for cramps.

So, if you're a cramped-up, weak-chested farter, this is the one for you.

The famous Bombay duck almost
disappeared from British curry house
menus when Brussels bureaucrats
banned vital fish imports from India.
The embargo was lifted when it was
agreed that only fish from
EU-approved processing plants in
India could be imported.

A FEW THINGS THAT MIGHT TURN UP ON A CURRY HOUSE MENU

R is for . . .

Rai	mustard
Raita	yoghurt-based dish
Raan	lamb

Everyone remembers Baloo the bear in Disney's *The Jungle Book* cracking open a coconut on his bonce, but the bare necessity he drank from it was not coconut milk. Coconut milk, widely used in curry cuisine, is extracted from the flesh of the coconut. What Baloo drank was coconut water.

Curry Is Good For You!

Spices that are positively healthy

Coriander – immensely useful in Indian cooking, the seeds are most commonly ground to a powder but are sometimes used whole and the leaves are used as a decorative garnish as well as for flavouring.

Coriander leaves are rich in Vitamin C and are often used as an ingredient in cold and flu remedies as are the seeds which, if eaten in large amounts, can have a narcotic effect.

Also believed to be an aphrodisiac and used for making love potions.

HOT AND HORNY!
Sex And The Curry

Rice might at first seem about as sexy
as those socks you once wore for six
days (and unless it's cooked properly it
has a lot less flavour), but it is a
powerful symbol of fertility. That's why
they throw rice at weddings – to wish
the happy couple a fertile union and to
remind the groom to change his socks
once in a while.

The Ripali restaurant in Palmer's Green, North London has developed a surprising line in takeaway deliveries, supplying customers as far away as Turkey, Spain and Canada via DHL. It all started when a regular customer who had been posted to Moscow on business came home on leave gasping for a curry. When he had to go back to Moscow, his luggage included a £700 takeaway.

A FEW THINGS THAT MIGHT TURN UP ON A CURRY HOUSE MENU

S is for . . .

Sag	spinach
Sonf	fennel
Samosa	pasty

Traditionally, Brits drink lager with their curry, but it does tend to fizz and pop a bit down below and, frankly, you may well have enough of that sort of thing brewing anyway. Indians are most likely to drink water and more likely to drink it once they have finished eating. Drinking water whilst eating a curry can actually make it seem hotter.

According to ancient Indian sayings, eat curry and you will go on for a hundred years. For some of us though, a century of Bombay Bum would just be too much to bear.

CURRY IS GOOD FOR YOU!

Spices that are positively healthy

Cinnamon – used both whole or ground, cinnamon comes from the bark of the cinnamon tree. If you find a stick of cinnamon in your Korma, don't eat it, it's just there for the flavouring.

Cinnamon has antiseptic properties, so it's good for treating wounds but it can also be made into a kind of tea which is good for diarrhoea and also helps with colds and chills.

Balti cooking, thought by many to
originate in Baltistan, actually comes from
the mountainous areas of North Pakistan
and was introduced into the UK via
Sparkhill and Sparkbrook in Birmingham
some ten years ago.

A FEW THINGS THAT MIGHT TURN UP ON A CURRY HOUSE MENU

T is for . . .

Tikka	marinated
Tejpatta	bay leaf
Tarka	seasoned oil

CURRY IS GOOD FOR YOU!

Spices that are positively healthy

Bay leaves – another essential ingredient ground into the ubiquitous garam masala, bay leaves are also used whole as a garnish or flavouring.

Although not known for being greatly beneficial to the health when eaten, bay leaves are commonly used in oils for soothing massage. Having a meat dopiaza rubbed into your back isn't really the same thing.

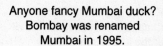

Anyone fancy Mumbai duck?
Bombay was renamed
Mumbai in 1995.

Patak's pappadams, produced in
Madras, are packaged for the UK and
Europe in Brechin in Scotland. They
arrive in Brechin in 16-tonne
consignments.
You'd need a lot of lime pickle
to get through that lot.

CURRY IS GOOD FOR YOU!

Spices that are positively healthy

Cloves – although they look like little nails (clove comes from *clavus*, Latin for nail), cloves are actually flower buds picked before they open and then dried.

Although used as an antiseptic and even an antibiotic, the best thing about cloves is that they have an anaesthetic property. Toothache driving you crazy? A couple of cloves placed on the tooth or gum and chewed now and again will help to ease the pain.

'The Less Gassy More Classy
Curryholics Beer' is how Indian beer
Cobra advertises itself, the point being
that less gas makes you less bloated
and allows you to pack yourself out
with more curry and even more Cobra.
The beer has been so successful that,
like its great rival, Kingfisher, it is now
brewed in the UK and the man behind
Cobra, Karan Bilimoria has also
launched another lager, Swift. For
those who would rather drink wine with
their curry, Karan has also developed
red and white wines, General Billy's,
named after his father, a retired
Indian Army officer.

If Kingfisher and Cobra lagers just don't give you enough choice when it comes to an alcoholic accompaniment to your regular curry, then there are now a few other 'Indian' lagers to choose from including Indian Lancer, Bangla Beer and Lal Toofan. No doubt you'll want to give them a try, and why not? According to a recent survey by *Tandoori* magazine, 62% of us vindaloonies order beer with our curries, gulping down an amazing 84 million pints a year in curry houses.

A FEW THINGS THAT MIGHT TURN UP ON A CURRY HOUSE MENU

U is for . . .

Unday   egg

Urad   split
(as in urad dhal – split lentils
– not 'Let's urad the bill')

There's nothing more annoying than sitting down to a fine, belly bulging, trouser splitting feast of curry and having your ears assaulted by the sound of 80s disco music or 70s glam rock. You want a touch of Indian-type atmosphere, don't you? And you won't get that from Brotherhood of Man or The Village People – okay, so they *did* have an Indian but he was an Apache so that doesn't count. According to *Tandoori* magazine, however, curry house managers are responding to their customers' desires and over 70% of Indian restaurants now have Indian classical music playing gently in the background with Indian film music as a second choice. Now that's what I call music to pig out to.

HOT AND HORNY!
Sex And The Curry

Papaya may well turn up on your local
curry house menu and is thought to be a
natural contraceptive, although if the
Indians really think that, how come their
population is around 130 million and
rising? One assumes that you eat the
papaya rather than wearing it like some
bizarre condom.
On the other hand, maybe that's what the
Indians are doing wrong . . .

CURRY IS GOOD FOR YOU!

Spices that are positively healthy

Chillies – a major part of any curry and incredibly good for lager sales. Bite down on one of the more potent chillies and your first reaction will be to down at least two pints of lager straight off.

Chillies are known to be a good disinfectant and allowing chilli powder to burn slowly in a pan will fumigate a room. Eating too many can also clear a room but, despite their afterburner reputation, chillies are used in indigestion remedies and also as a cure for colds and fevers.

A concoction using chillies can also be used to rub on your head to strengthen the hair and stop you going bald.

Downtrodden? Disheartened? Depressed? You sound like a barrel of laughs. Get out and have a curry to cheer yourself up. Ginger, a common ingredient in curries, is believed to ease depression. Ask your doctor for a chicken tikka prescription.

A FEW THINGS THAT MIGHT TURN UP ON A CURRY HOUSE MENU

V is for . . .

Vindaloo   oh, come on, you
                must know by now . . .

Apart from the undoubted health benefits to be gained by eating curries, those clever Indians discovered centuries ago that their spices can help to stop food going bad in the various hot/dry/damp climates that exist on the sub-continent. Ginger, for example, has anti-bacterial properties that help to stop meat and fish from going off.

Many Indian recipes stem from texts 3,000 years old that advised of the medicinal and healing properties of different foods.

Rogan Josh may sound like some handsome, romantic Indian folk hero but it actually only means fat and hot. Rogan Josh is traditionally made using meat cooked in its own fat.

Korma, in its light-coloured creamy
sauce, was developed for Shah Jehan
(builder of the Taj Mahal) who hosted
all-white parties where everyone wore
white, there were white carpets,
white decorations, white flowers and
all the food served was white.
The parties were held by the light of
a full moon.

Tamarind – a sour flavouring for
chutneys, tamarind comes from the
fruit of the tamarind tree.
Gargling with just a little tamarind
mixed with water can help to soothe a
sore throat but it can become
quite addictive and too much
can *give* you a sore throat, too.

Although your average dhansak
generally contains chicken, lamb or
prawn the term actually comes from
Parsee Gujerati and means rice (dhan)
and vegetables (sak).

A FEW THINGS THAT MIGHT TURN UP ON A CURRY HOUSE MENU

W is for . . .

Why not skip W, and X and Y for that matter, as you're about as likely to see words beginning with these letters as you are to pick up an unbroken pappadam using only a claw hammer and a loofa.

If you thought that Bhuna must be somewhere in India, then you were wrong. Don't you ever guess these things correctly? Bhuna refers to the way the dish is stir-fried.

Tomatoes turn up in so many Indian recipes you'd have thought they were native to India, but they were actually introduced by the Portuguese in the 16th century.

Many Indian cooks will not prepare
dishes using meat when there is a new
or full moon.

CURRY IS GOOD FOR YOU!

Spices that are positively healthy

Cardamom – large and small cardamoms are an extremely common ingredient in Indian cookery. They are used in every garam masala mixture and the large ones may appear whole in your biryani. Set them aside, they're not meant to be eaten.

Chewing cardamom seeds will help to freshen your mouth if you are having a particularly nasty post-curry bad breath day.

Rice goes with curry like love and marriage, horse and carriage, moon and June (although moon can also go with 30 days suspended and a £100 fine) but the choicest of rice is Basmati. It has longer grains and a wonderful aroma, although it is usually more expensive than other rice.

A FEW THINGS THAT MIGHT TURN UP ON A CURRY HOUSE MENU

Z is for . . .

Zafran	saffron
Zeera	cumin
Zarda	a dessert with rice and nuts

Kulfi – Indian ice cream – the best way to finish off a curry and the best way to end this book. Traditionally, kulfi-wallahs made their ice cream without the help of electric freezers. The mixture was poured into metal containers and agitated or churned until it set hard.

About the Author

Rod Green is a retired astronaut who applied to join NASA's Mars space programme after a bloke down the pub told him that the polar ice caps there were actually frozen lager.
He left NASA on discovering that being sealed into a spacesuit is the last thing you want the morning after a mighty vindaloo.

He lives in Surrey with his wife and son and a mounting overdraft.